Getting Here

the poems

Alice Cline

BookLeaf Publishing
India | USA | UK

Made with ❤ on the BookLeaf Publishing Platform
www.bookleafpub.in
www.bookleafpub.com

Dedication

Dedicated to everyone who gives too much.

Preface

We all do the best we can with the knowledge and experience we have. Sometimes our knowledge and experience isn't enough to stop us from making choices and relationships that cut us deep and leave scars to remind us of wrong turns. However, there is strength that comes from the endurance of pain. Wisdom to always move forward.

Acknowledgements

I would like to acknowledge my best friends. The ones that become family, and stick around through all the chaos of life and provide unconditional love and support. To the people that didn't leave through the darkness and helped me find the light again. I love you all.

1. Sinking

The world is spinning faster and faster, the ground tilts.
All slips further from my grasp.
The ground envelops me, as my body wilts.
My screams are nothing more than a whispered rasp.
My skin takes root and digs in deep.
I sink deeper, further from the cool breeze.
The soil moistens as I weep.
My lungs take in the muck; making me wheeze.
The wet silt cools my face.
I settle into the protective cocoon.
Ease my way into the earth's embrace.
The holds so tight, I swoon.
I hear lives walking over me.
The truth is stark.
My prison sets me free.
No need to close my eyes, for its already dark.

2. Small town

I really do hate this place,
Always turning around and seeing the same old face.
Everyone tries to draw you in with a smile that is really a sneer,
They try to hide it but it's crystal clear.
I will not be trapped in this place,
Soon I will be gone without a trace.

3. Tears

I fill up with tears from my toes to just under my eye;
Bones soaked through but I can't cry.
Vibrations burn my finger tips;
Please, tears come...quench my lips.

4. Shards

I see myself as I am looking from the skies,
I see everything in the depths of my eyes.
The shards of my face catch bits of light,
Through the shattered pieces shine none too bright.
Though the edges cut like a boat in a river,
My eyes are steadfast and do not quiver.
Behind my eyes is something screaming in sorrow,
But also hope for a happier tomorrow.
I see there are many things for my eyes to share,
I see my soul laid bare.
They would see love, faith and passion,
Given wholly in the most beautiful fashion.
Those eyes of mine will keep their steady gaze,
Never failing, no matter the days.
Though a tear may escape and drip from a shard,
My heart will hold fast and cling hard.
Someday I will figure out how to put the pieces back in place,
And there will be strength behind my face.

5. Darkness

Tears kiss lips as they drip from eyelashes.
Salty and sweet, tear and tongue clashes.
Chest heaves as breath is chased.
From the corner of the mind, a monster is faced.
Heart pounds to a rhythm, all its own.
Body sends shivers straight to the bone.
Color drains from all seen.
Running through a black tunnel, away from where you've been.
The world is mute as it suddenly tips.
Silence is a companion, its' venom now drips.
Heat melts the skin.
Liquid fire, from eyes to chin.
Infinity of darkness becomes the savior.
Soothing to the core.

6. Cycle

There is an ocean inside me.
The waves are large and almost black.
You can barely make them out against the midnight sky.
They crash into one another violently, never ceasing.
There is no one but me in the middle of the ocean.
No one to see the storm.
Sometimes I go under.
I become part of the stormy sea.
Under the surface the crashing gently rocks me back and forth.
I am calm.
Even though I don't want to, I must come up for air.
I must reach the surface again.
Involuntarily, I struggle to be where I belong.
Every once in a while, the sun shines, just when I think I can't say at the surface any longer it shines.
He makes the sun shine.
The man with the ever judging sky blue eyes that bore into my soul.
He douses me in an icy fire that warms my body and cools the raging storm.
He takes the struggle away.
I am allowed to rest while he takes my life into his hands.

I stay afloat without trying.
Though I try to make him stay, somehow I spark a once doused inferno within him, and he leaves.
Then I fall.
The comforting thrilling icy hot fire fades away...and I fall inside myself.
There is a darkness that I thought had left me.
The man with the misleading smile can give me hope then take it away.
He accuses, he attempts to pull me in the opposite direction I am so frantically trying to go.
I want him back, I yell, I plead, I stay quiet, I cry.
My tears become a raging sea. I am alone.
He does not understand that he is my everything.
I am thrown between the waves of my tears.
Praying the sun will come out once again.

7. Together

Hungry winds and desperate rain,
Driving hard as they came.
Rhythmically trees dance,
Putting the world in a calming trance.
Drops hit the window one by one,
Harder, harder till the dance is done..
Thunder rolls through the sky,
On and on like a sweet lullaby.
Lightning strikes and lights the dark,
Spewing fire when it hits it's mark.
Happening apart yet still together,
Violent, beautiful, calming, forever.

8. Liar

Does it make me a liar?

That all I want to do is move on from you?
That I don't believe anymore that you have the perfect heart?

Does it make me a liar?

That I can't believe your love was pure and true?
That I never want to be together, but always apart?

Does it make me a liar?

That I'm ok with running to someone else's bed?
That I want to erase the memory of your touch?

Does it make me a liar?

That I'm not cursed with happy memories, but tainted ones instead?
That this kind of betrayal is too much?

Does it make me a liar?

You omitted parts of your mind.
And now everything is unclear.
Fuck it, omission is deceit.
I'm not the liar here.

9. Forward

Take another step
The pain makes me scream
Take another step
I can't breathe
Take another step
The noise can't escape
Take another step
The world is barren
Take another step

10. Again

I'm falling fast.
I do that.
It hasn't ended well.
I thought it wouldn't happen again.
That easy feeling.
That I want everything feeling.

11. Burned

I give myself too readily
Too easily
But somehow it's never enough.
My thoughts and my cares,
My thighs,
I just want reciprocation.
It's too much I'm too much,
To hard to handle,
I'm never really the priority that sticks.
Over and over I jump into the burning building.
And I'm shocked when I'm burned.
I can't breathe
I can't let tears go,
I've felt the sizzling pains too many times.
When will someone jump in after me?

12. I am...

I'm sinking
Tired of fighting the pull.
I found my voice but it's fading.

I'm tired
Sneak attacks come in waves.
Sleep never comes because I'm wired

I'm sneaking through life
Covering the glass shards beneath me.
They tear and pull at me under the surface.

I'm covered.
Bloody with salt in my wounds
Pulled under, cut through and smothered.

13. Maybe

I feel like running.
Like I need to fight.
Something is coming.
It's just out of sight.

Barriers should be going up.
And a moat should be dug.
Thoughts move like syrup.
Sticky, suffocating cracks like a plug.

You deserve better.
I deserve to be hurt.
There is so much pressure.
I'll never get to the dessert.

But I can't move.
I want this so bad.
Maybe this time I won't lose.
Maybe this love won't make me sad.

14. Caution

All the pain has built up like tiny grains of powder.
Each grain is soft and inconsequential.
Each one means nothing.
Each one means everything.

They are constantly shifting with each step I take.
Every thought I have makes a ripple through.
I get motion sickness.
The movement makes me dizzy and suspicious.

They slide over and over one another.
Chafing each surface.
Friction is causing static.
The waves are becoming more erratic.

Sparks are surprising
They are hard to snuff out.
I have trouble keeping up and stopping the spread.
It may ignite what I dread.

Too much heat
And they will all spill out.
A landslide of fear and worry rushing to the ground.
It will suffocate anything and everyone around.

15. Sky

I want to wrap myself in the sky.
To be surrounded by the deepening colors.
Pink, glowing orange
Lavender haze turns blue
Stuck in the middle, a river of seafoam.
If only I could lay in it, feel the cool warm comfort,
I want to wrap myself in the sky.

16. Always

It hurts.
It always hurts.
Happiness is never enough.
I don't know how to be happy.
I give power to time.
To looks of disgust.
It hurts.
It always hurts.
One wrong move
I question everything.
I give power to thoughts.
To lost emotions.
It hurts.
It always hurts.

17. Bitter

Bitterness it seeps in.
All where I have been.
I used to think it had purpose.
That maybe it paved the way.
But still I'm really alone.
Second best to a fucking phone.

18. Family

Blood is thicker than water
They say
Because blood is thick
And sticky
They say but you're the daughter

What about those that choose
I say
Not because they have to
But want
In your life they infuse

19. Abomination

You shouldn't be here,
You're created out of sin.

Deceit and lies brought you to life,
You're like a train wreck bringing strife.

Bad daughter, bad friend,
Your always the loose end.

Fuck what's said.

I am not an abomination,
I'll take care of my own salvation.

20. Unconditional

I love easily.
I can feel the unconditional weight of it.
It pushes in from all sided.

I love easily.
I can feel myself slipping away.
Swallowed whole.

I love easily.
I can feel the confusion settle in.
Where am I?

21. Hack

A laugh can take a turn
Hysterics can be a fake

Words can’t be taken back
Miscommunicating hack

Listening to more than speech
Body displays the breach

www.ingramcontent.com/pod-product-compliance
Lightning Source LLC
Chambersburg PA
CBHW051756130826
49812CB00033B/1180
9789370923430